Siam Sinfonietta: Internationally Acclaimed Youth Symphony Orchestra

by the staff of Bangkok Opera Foundation
edited by S.P. Somtow

published by Diplodocus Press
Second Edition
© 2018, 2025 Bangkok Opera Foundation

ISBN: 978-0-9900142-9-4

9 8 7 6 5 4 3 2 1

*Klementinum, Prague*
*A church where Mozart himself performed*

# Siam Sinfonietta
## Thailand's internationally recognized youth ensemble

Founded in 2010 by European Cultural Achievement Award Laureate and Thailand National Artist and Public Diplomacy Awardee Somtow Sucharitkul, the Siam Sinfonietta was designed to create world-class classical musicians from the most talented young Thai performers. Using a radical new holistic approach to teaching music, the "Somtow Method" does not replace traditional music pedagogy but supplements it by constantly challenging students to ask "why" in addition to "how."

This results in absorption of the entire context of classical music — historical, cultural, and interpretational. The method has proved itself thoroughly — in its first international competition, the *Summa Cum Laude* in Vienna's famed *Musikverein*, the orchestra won the very first first prize ever granted a Thai symphony orchestra. It has gone on to win many more top prizes, three in festivals in *Carnegie Hall*. Graduates of the program are acknowledged as some of the finest young musicians in the region.

The Sinfonietta project is one of the most successful educational experiments of the Twenty-first Century, and was recently subject of a much-lauded dissertation in Hungary.

In each of the orchestra's ten European tours so far, the Siam Sinfonietta has played to completely packed audiences, as witness the photograph *below* of the Prinz Regententheater on Munich on the evening of a concert that featured Mahler's First Symphony, the Suriyothai Suite, and Love Songs by H.M. King Rama IX of Thailand.

The orchestra's recent achievements include starring in the award-winning film *The Maestro: A Symphony of Terror* and being featured in the Oscar-nominated *Tár* with Cate Blanchett and the musician *Dream!*. They're the official orchestra of the Oldenburg Film Festival in

*An internationally acclaimed, radical program for fast-tracking young Thai musicians to realize their highest potential*

Performance of Beethoven's Ninth at the ceremony naming Somtow Sucharitkul as a laureate of the European Cultural Achievement Award, presented by the KulturForum Europa Berlin.

The concert itself was, in the words of Michael Proudfoot, reviewer from London's Opera magazine, "an amazing performance. It is impossible to believe that the Siam Sinfonietta is a youth orchestra, so polished is their playing." Proudfoot compared Somtow's reading of the symphony with the legendary Furtwängler's interpretation from the first half of the twentieth century.

Of the Sinfonietta's The Ring in Ninety Minutes, musicologist J.P. Kirkland said, "a glorious sound, these young and brilliant musicians seeming to enjoy every moment of the score in front of them and capturing with significant eloquence the delicate balance between the highly dramatic, often loud passages and the lyrical quieter sections."

"The Sinfonietta played with panache and precision. About five times during the evening, the concert was interrupted by a thunderous standing ovation."
— *Bangkok Post*

"I was energized by the level of excitement those kids brought to their playing!"
— *Viswa Subbaraman*

*First Thai symphony orchestra to win first prize in a world-class international competition: Golden Hall of the Musikverein, Vienna, 2012*

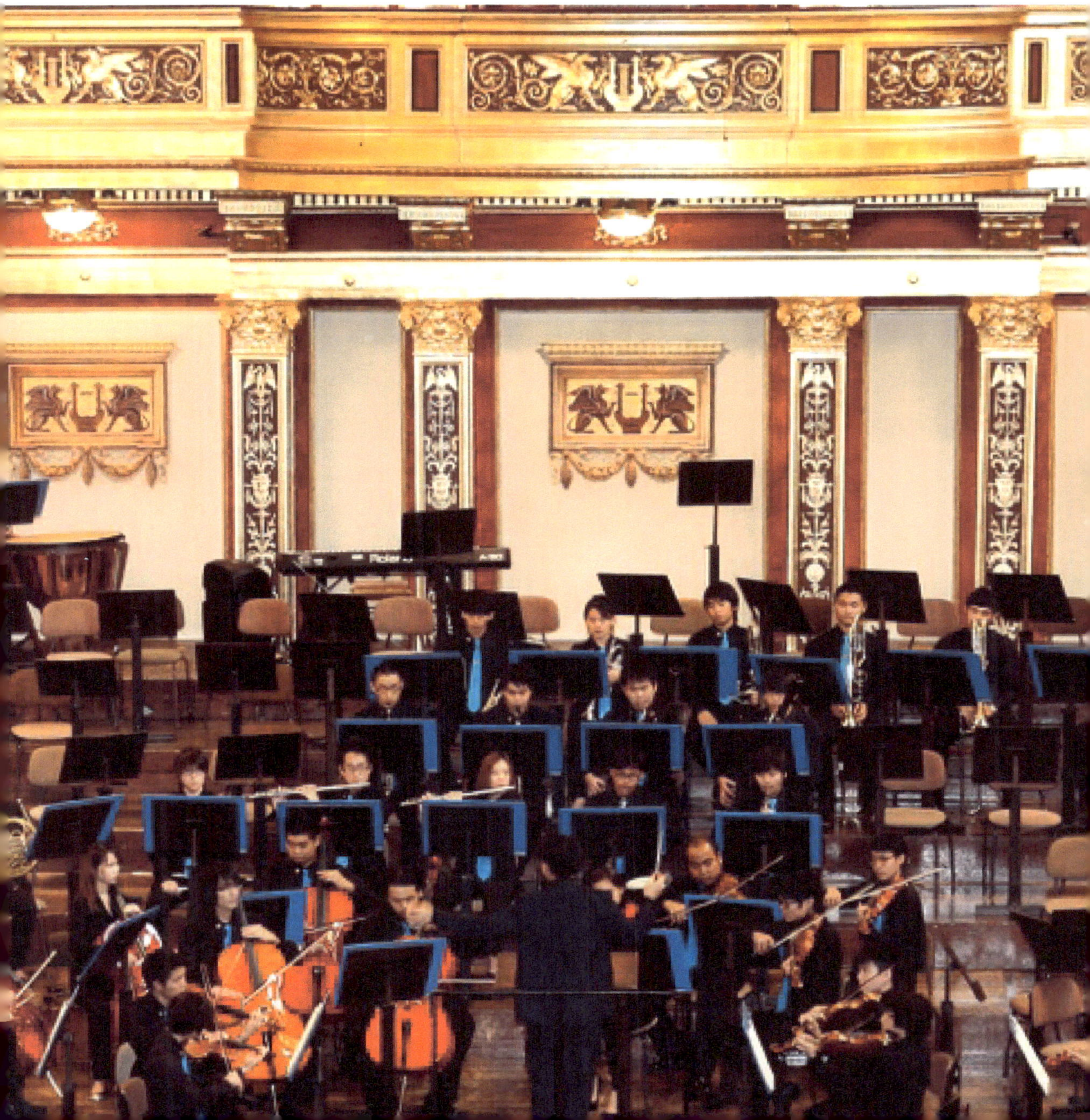

*created by*
*European Cultural Achievement*
*Award Laureate*
*Somtow Sucharitkul*

*Thailand's internationally acclaimed youth orchestra*

*First Prize, Summa Cum Laude Festival, Vienna*
*Gold Award, Los Angeles International Music Festival*
*Gold Prize, New York International Music Festival Carnegie Hall*
*Gold Prize, Sounds of Summer Festival, Carnegie Hall*
*Golden Showcase Award, Sounds of Spring Festival, Carnegie Hall*

Invited to open International Classical Music Festival. Johor Bahru
First Thai Orchestra ever invited to Europa Fest, Berlin
Sold-out concerts in Cuvilíes Theater and Prinz Regenthentheater Munich
Twice special guests at Young Artists Festival Bayreuth
Frequent appearances in Czech Republic, Germany, and first Thai symphony orchestra to tour the Middle East

Collaborated with Opera Siam to become the first youth orchestra in the region to play a full opera alongside world-class opera singers

Pioneered populist concerts such as the *Star Wars Ultimate Symphony Concert, Harry Potter and his Magical Friends,* and the *Princess Concert*

First orchestra in Thailand to give public performances of major repertoire works like *The Rite of Spring,* Mahler's 9th and 6th Symphonies, Bartok's *Miraculous Mandarin* and other major works.

**The Siam Sinfonietta project is a 100% scholarship program. The members are chosen through a rigorous audition annually and membership does not automatically extend beyond one year without audition. Instruction from international artists, national and international touring, and all the costs of training the musicians are borne by sponsors, government, corporate or individual.**

*Annual Mahler camp in Pattaya*

## Siam Sinfonietta's special relationship with Gustav Mahler

When Siam Sinfonietta won first prize in Vienna in 2012, one of its showcase pieces was a new reconstruction of the *Purgatorio* movement from Mahler's Tenth Symphony, recreated from Mahler's pencil sketches by Somtow Sucharitkul, who is known for conducting the first complete Mahler cycle in Southeast Asia. The judges remarked that the rendition "really sounded like Mahler" and since then Siam Sinfonietta has performed more Mahler symphonies than most other youth ensembles, including No. 4, No. 5, No. 9. and performances in the Konzerthaus Berlin, Prinz Regententheater Munich and in Dresden of No. 1 which all brought standing ovations.

*Siam Sinfonietta at Mahler's birthplace*

Most recently, the Sinfonietta performed No. 6. Mahler Society musicologist Jean-Pierre Kirkland's review in the *Post* said:

"What was so amazing was the fact that the strength and forcefulness of youth was able to capture the terrifying journey through *'angst und stürm'* — anxiety and turmoil of the most penetrating kind — which are the hallmarks of this enigmatic work."

These young musicians' reading of Mahler is recognized as a very special relationship. Of their performance of No. 1, Somtow said: "When we were touring in Czechia, I took the kids to the forest near the village of Kaliště where Mahler was born. I explained to them that when Mahler writes the direction *like a sound of nature,* it's the sound of *this* forest."

This teaching by *context*, by complete immersion in the culture, history, psychology and rich background of classical music is the essence of the Somtow method, which gives young musicians the edge they need to excel.

*Siam Sinfonietta at St. Stephen's Cathedral Vienna, Summa Cum Laude*

Siam Sinfonietta was the first Thai symphony orchestra to tour the United States and has performed in Disney Hall, Los Angeles, the Birch Theater, San Diego and several other California locations. It was also the first Thai symphony orchestra to play in Carnegie Hall, where it has performed three times.

Each program at Carnegie was a cunningly crafted blend of Thai and American composers. Works by H.M. King Rama IX were performed each time. Works by Trisdee na Patalung and Somtow Sucharitkul were also premiered including the world premieres of Trisdee's *Moha* and excerpts from Somtow's *DasJati* series. The orchestra performed great American compositions such as an excerpt from Daron Hagen's opera *Amelia* (in fact the New York premiere), *Three Places in New England* by Charles Ives, Aaron Copland's *Appalachian Spring,* as well as standard classical repertoire works.

## *The Somtow Method*

This revolution in approach to musical education brings an added dimension to the understanding of music and personal development. The method concentrates on context, culture, and historical background in order to lead students to an enhanced understanding of what they do, adding an extra "edge" to what they learn through traditional music pedagogy. It is not a replacement for regular teaching but a value-added expansion that has had proven results and is endorsed by many top educators and musicians.

Each year the Bangkok Opera Foundation's Educational Program seeks out the best young musicians by audition. Students must audition every year; acceptance does not imply automatic annual renewal.

The acceptance of students into the program is on a 100% scholarship basis. The investment in each student each year is approximately 100,000 baht with an additional 50,000 - 100,000 for each student taken on an international tour or competition. We do not charge *anything* to the students or their parents in order to ensure that all are eligible regardless of financial status.

The lessons learned through their time in the educational program gives young people advantages in their future education and their careers, and also in creating a balanced way of of living in which art and life are intimately connected and enhance one another.

*Siam Sinfonietta in Berlin*

## Y? The Basic Principles of the Somtow Method

In the early years of the twenty-first century, a fifteen-year-old prodigy named Trisdee na Patalung came up to Somtow Sucharitkul, who was attending a concert in the Goethe Institute in Bangkok. Trisdee said, "I want to be a composer." Somtow asked him if he had anything to show, and Trisdee pulled out one of his compositions from his backpack.

Somtow said, "It was a Chopin-style polonaise, but the melody was in Northeastern Thai *Isaan* style. It was apparent to me that Trisdee was a genius, because even with the tiny amount of raw material he possessed, he was being playful — a sure sign of brilliance." He told Trisdee he would teach him himself. "Other teachers will tell you the things you can't do — the *rules*. I will teach you what you *can* do."

In the ten years in which Somtow directly engaged Trisdee's talent and in which most of the most gifted young musicians in the country started to drift towards this new creative center of gravity, Somtow evolved the principles which were to become the Somtow method.

The first principle was to seek to answer the question *WHY*. Traditional music teaching often concentrates on *HOW* — the way to make the sound you want to make from your chosen instrument.

Answering *WHY* gives a rich, contextual mass of data that envelops your interpretation and gives you the edge to play the music with a thought-out interpretation and with real understanding.

With *WHY* as the basic impetus, this method is not a *mass training system* like the Suzuki Method or El Sistema. It is, rather, a highly individualized and interactive way of teaching that requires great personal commitment from both student and teacher.

Somtow's process towards an interpretation is a progression of five steps, each of them easily remembered as "The Five C's".

**CHAOS**: Where everything begins. It is important not to fear chaos, because all art starts with the artist's attempt to find meaning in chaos.

**CONNECTION**: Chaos begins to resolve when the artist starts to see connections between pieces of the chaos.

**CONTEXT**: Around the kernels of the connected pieces, context begins to grow, enriching the understanding.

**COMPLEXITY**: Context enlarges the field of vision; complexity adds layers of meaning: emotive, historic, psychological. The artistic vision grows both horizontally and vertically, becoming three-dimensional.

**COURAGE**: Once the interpretation is built, there comes the "moment of truth": you must have the courage to speak out.

These steps lead to:

**COMMUNICATION**: This is why you chose to be an artist. You have something to stay. Communication also follows a fivefold path"

1. Have something say.
2. Say it.
3. Be prepared to master all the technical skills needed to say exactly what you wanted to say.
4. Follow your truth, no matter where it leads you. Accept the consequences.
5. Remember that, in the split second of creation, you are the only one in the universe with the power to say what you must say. Take a deep breath and "save the universe."

*Siam Sinfonietta in Thailand Cultural Center, in Munich, and in Los Angeles.*

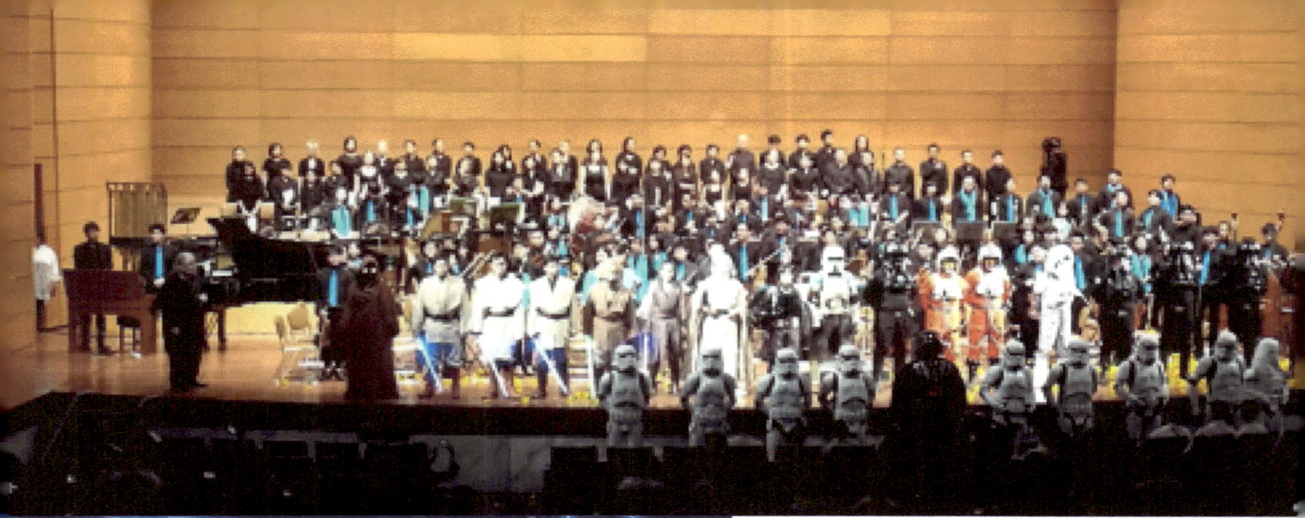

# Popular Outreach

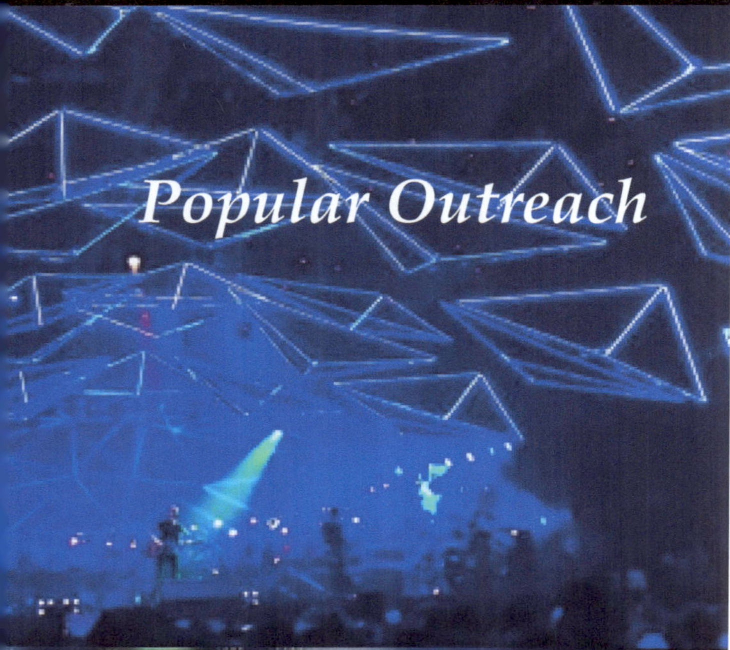

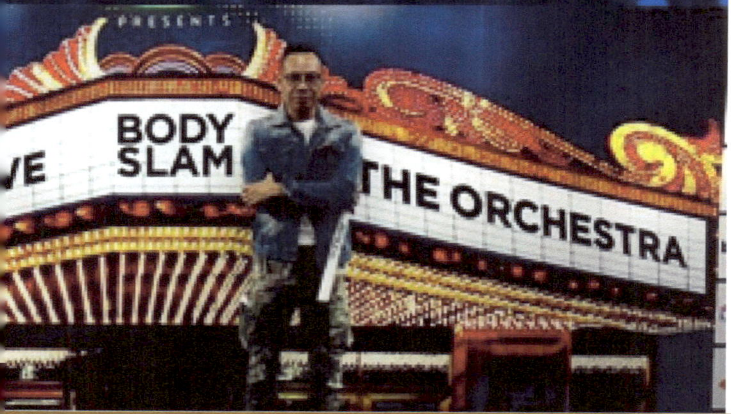

**above**

Siam Sinfonietta in Thailand Cultural Center, performs the first "epic Star Wars symphony concert" in the region with music from all nine of the Star Wars movies released thus far

**left**

a pioneering fusion of Thai pop/rock from high popular artist Bodyslam with new arrangements for orchestra created by Trisdee na Patalung

**below**

The success of the Star Wars concert was followed by the first all=Harry Potter concert in Thailand.

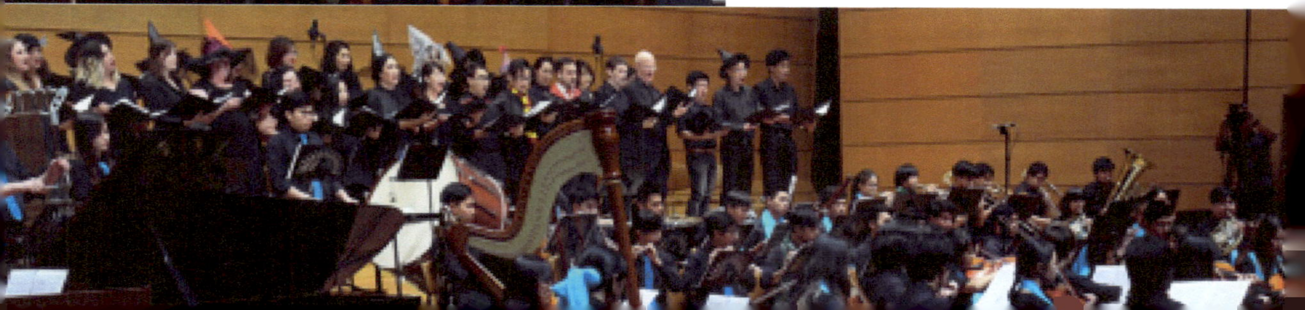

## *International Cooperation*

Vital to Siam Sinfonietta's and YSP's development are the relationships with the world's top performing entities.

Each year, the Sinfonietta has a camp in which members of the Bayreuth Festival Orchestra teach the ins and outs of the hardest operatic repertoire. They have also had training sessions with the orchestra of the Deutsche Oper Berlin, with Min Yang of the London Symphony Orchestra, and Vilmos Olah, concertmaster of the Hungarian Radio Orchestra.

Each year, the Sinfonietta goes on at least one international tour or competition, which has made it one of Thailand's most recognized cultural ambassadors  The orchestra has played to standing ovations in the Prinz Regentheater and Cuvillies Theater in Munich, the Konzerthaus Berlin, the Bayreuth Youth Festival, the Brno Opera, the Emirates Palace in Abu Dhabi, Disney Hall in California, Carnegie Hall, the Musikverein and Konzerthaus of Vienna … They also perform regularly in Chiangmai, Korat, Yala, Hua Hin … all over Thailand.

Collaborations have taken place with ensembles from Taiwan, Malaysia, and many European countries.

**below**
*The Siam Sinfonietta rehearses in Disney Hall, one of the world's most technologically advanced performing venues.*

**right**

*poster advertising the Siam Sinfonietta in the Czech Republic*

**below**

*at the Young Euro Classic Festival in Berlin, in the famed Berlin Konzerthaus, performing a program of music by King Rama IX of Thailand, Somtow Sucharitkul, and Mahler's First Symphony*

**left**

*At the Klementinum, Prague*

**below right**

*At the Emirates Palae in Abu Dhabi*

**below left**

*Konzerthaus in Vienna, Austrai*

**right**

*with Czech pianist Jan Bartoš in Beethoven's Emperor Concerto*

**left**

*Nancy Yuen performing the soprano solo in Mahler's Fourth Symphony with the Sinfonietta*

**above and below**

*performing in a memorial ceremony for the victims of the Japan tsunami, with the governor of Bangkok, in front of the Town Hall*

## From Ambassadorial Residences to Palaces to Street Fairs

Photographs of Siam Sinfonietta from French Embassy *Loy Kratong* reception; the audience from the Thai Festival in Bad Homburg, Germany; Mrigadayavan Palace in Hua Hin where the Siam Sinfonietta goes to perform frequently; Minoritenkirche in Vienna, Austra

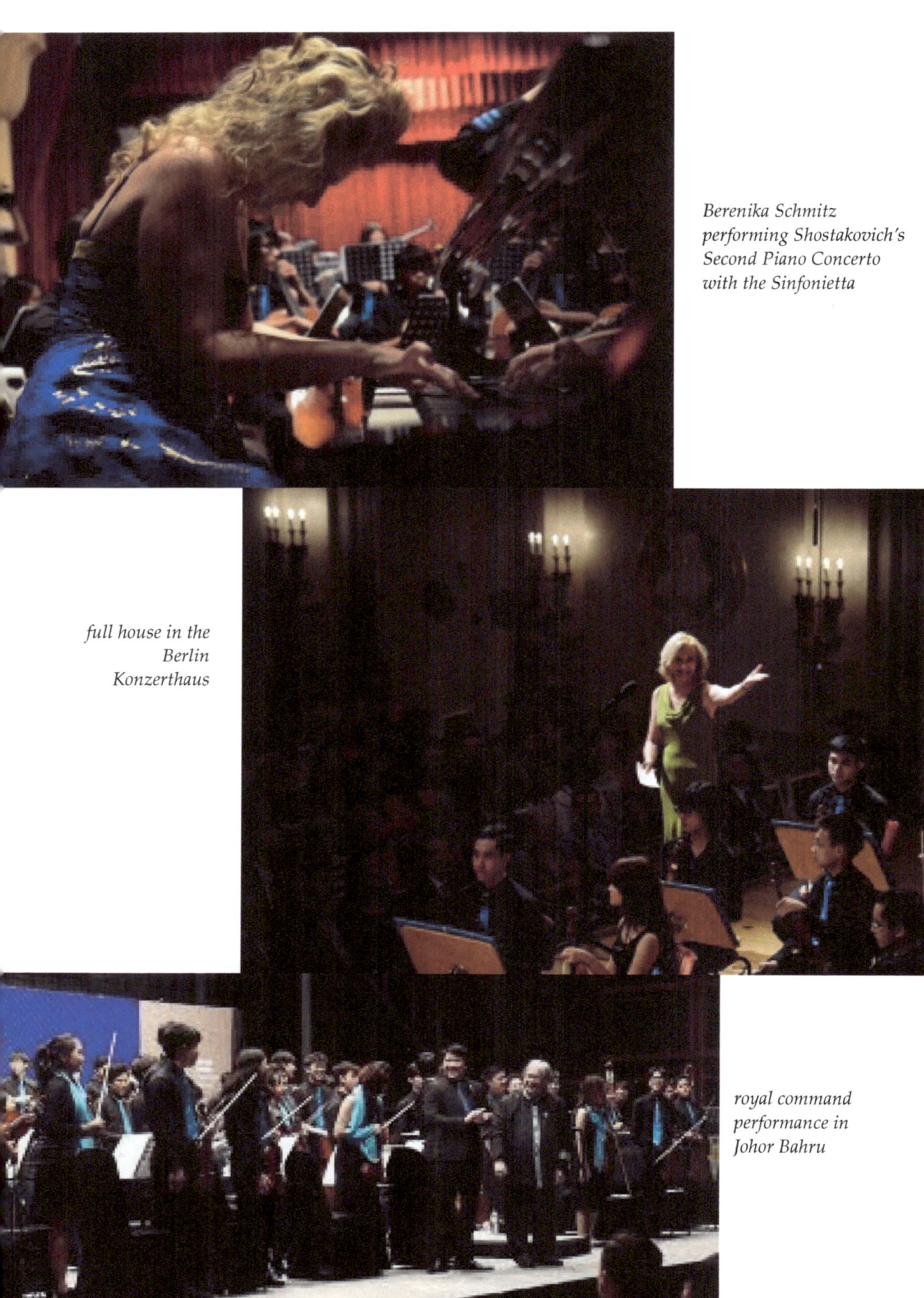

*Berenika Schmitz performing Shostakovich's Second Piano Concerto with the Sinfonietta*

*full house in the Berlin Konzerthaus*

*royal command performance in Johor Bahru*

# Opera and Siam Sinfonietta

Being part of the educational division of an opera company, Siam Sinfonietta is frequently involved in opera production, both fully professional performances with world-class soloists and with the Young Soloists Program.

Opera Siam is Thailand's flagship opera company and the Young Soloist Program was created to develop Thai singers for international careers. The singers work with international coaches such as Richard Harrell, head of opera at San Francisco Conservatory, Hans Niewenhuis, director of the Netherlands Opera Studio, and Damian Whiteley, leading opera coach of the Zurich Opera. They perform comprimario roles in Opera Siam productions studying their art alongside

**above**

*poster advertising The Silent Prince in Brno, Czechia*

**right**

*a scene from The Silent Prince, Sinfonietta and Young Soloists Program*

The Silent Prince

visiting international opera stars such as Phillip Joll of Covent Garden, Michael Chance, artistic director of the Grange Park Opera, Nancy Yuen, artistic director of Singapore Lyric Opera, and many others. Graduates of the YSP have gone on to careers in Europe and the United States. The junior division of this group produces a children's opera each year, most recently "Brundibar" and "The Happy Prince."

In 2018, the Sinfonietta had its first chance to play for a major opera performance with top international singers: a new production of *Madama Butterfly*

Previous operas include *Brundibar, The Happy Prince, The Diary of Anne Frank.*

2018 will see the Sinfonietta play for an opera that none of the professional operas in Thailand have yet dared to perform: Strauss's *Salome.*

*three opera productions that have involved the participation of the Siam Sinfonietta*

# Royal Anthem Project

*Korat*

The brainchild of HSH Prince Chatrichalerm Yugala, the project to create a massive performance of the Thai Royal Anthem in memory of the late King Rama IX was one of the historic events in Thai history.

An estimated 300,000 people gathered to sing the Royal Anthem in Sanam Luang in Bangkok, and equally large numbers in Thailand's Northeastern metropolis of Korat and in the southern city of Yala. It was the Siam Sinfonietta who formed the core of the orchestra along with numerous friends and associates forming an orchestra of over 300 people to accompany this huge ensemble.

*Bangkok*

**above**

*The Royal Anthem in Korat*

**right**

*Sanam Luang filled with an estimated 300,000 participants*

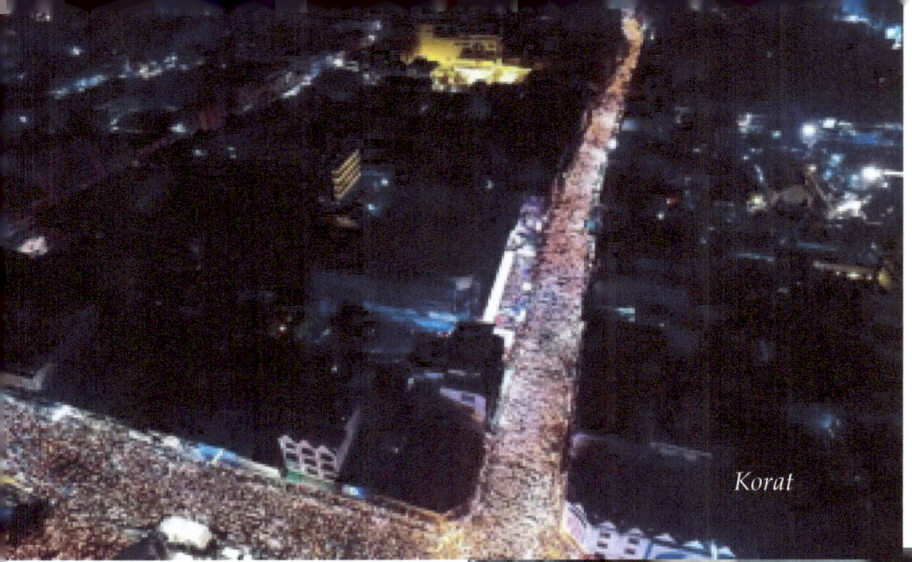

**left**

*performance by night of the Royal Anthem in the city of Korat literally overflowed the square and filled several major streets.*

*Korat*

**below**

*performances in Yala included an amazing crowd-painting of a white elephant presented*

*Yala*

*Yala*

**above and left**

The Sinfonietta plays for the Royal Anthem memorial event at Sanamluang in Bangkok

**above far left**

in Korat, the anthem took place during pouring rain: immensely moving

**right**

The Sinfonietta plays for a Royal Anthem memorial event at the headquarters of Shell

## Siam Sinfonietta Events special relationships in local Thai communities

**Community Outreach**

*Explaining the orchestra to children in Phuket* — since 2021, regular performances for audiences and young people in Phuket

*Music festival in Koh Chang* — first time in 2024, new annual music festival in Koh Chang

*performances at Wat Arun* — in collaboration with Thai Group, performances to highlight Wat Arun

*Sounder Festival in Korat* — for the past ten years, regular performances for youth, and special workshops for young musicians in Korat

# Siam Sinfonietta in Film

Siam Sinfonietta was featured in the Oscar-nominated film *Tár* starring Cate Blanchett and played a major role in *The Maestro,* a Thai film which won over forty international awards.

Invited to appear at the Oldenburg Film Festival to perform music from *The Maestro,* the Siam Sinfonietta became the official orchestra of the festival and travels to Germany regularly to perform there.

## Past Sponsors of Siam Sinfonietta Projects

Singha Corporation
AIS
PTT
Tourist Authority of Thailand
Bangkok Metropolitan Authority
Ministry of Culture
Department of Cultural Promotion
Office of Contemporary Art and Culture
Daimler Benz
ThaiBev
Goethe Institut
Arnoma Hotel
Banyan Tree Hotel
Kempsinski Hotel
John F. Kennedy Foundation
Anonymous
Crown Property Bureau
Embassy of Czech Republic
Embassy of Republic of Germany
Embassy of Slovakia
Embassy of Republic of Ireland
Embassy of Israel
Embassy of Australia
Embassy of the United Kingdom
Embassy of Italy
Embassy of Hungary
Embassy of Austria
Dr. Sompong Sucharitkul
Mr. Yos Euarchukiati
ABRSM
EuroAsia
Young Euro Classic

Young Artists Festival Bayreuth
Mr. Joachim Horn
Thomastik-Infeld Vienna
Old England Students Association
Asavanant Dental Clinic
Rembrandt Hotel
Thai Yarnyon
Thai Airways International
Etihad
Royal Thai Embassy, Berlin
Royal Thai Embassy, Prague
Royal Thai Embassy, Washington DC
Mission of Thailand to the United Nations
Royal Thai Embassy, Abu Dhabi
Royal Thai Embassy, Kuala Lumpur
Rangsit University
Chulalongkorn University
Siam Commercial Bank
Bangkok Bank
Hemaraj
Bangkok Art and Culture Center
Yamaha
The Mall Group
Nakorn Rachasima Cultural Department
Emirates Palace Hotel
Dr. Paul Beresford-Hill
The Mountbatten Foundation
Festa Musicale
Khunying Barbara Riepl
Mr. Joerg Ayrle
Mr. Ho Kwon Ping

www.ingramcontent.com/pod-product-compliance
Lightning Source LLC
Chambersburg PA
CBHW041438010526
44118CB00002B/112